BIOGRAPHIES

John Singer Sargent

The Life of an Artist

Eshel Kreiter

Marc Zabludoff

 Enslow Publishers, Inc.

40 Industrial Road   PO Box 38
Box 398   Aldershot
Berkeley Heights, NJ 07922   Hants GU12 6BP
USA   UK

http://www.enslow.com

John Singer Sargent

Library of Congress Cataloging-in-Publication Data
Kreiter, Eshel.
  John Singer Sargent : the life of an artist / Eshel Kreiter and Marc Zabludoff.
    p. cm. — (Artist Biographies)
Includes bibliographical references and index.
  ISBN 0-7660-1879-2
  1. Sargent, John Singer, 1856-1925—Juvenile literature. 2.
Painters—United States—Biography—Juvenile literature. [1. Sargent,
John Singer, 1856-1925. 2. Artists.] I. Zabludoff, Marc. II. Title.
III. Series.
  ND237.S3 K74 2002
  759.13—dc21

                                    2001001813

Printed in the United States of America
10 9 8 7 6 5 4 3 2 1

To Our Readers: We have done our best to make sure all Internet addresses in this book were active and appropriate when we went to press. However, the author and the publisher have no control over and assume no liability for the material available on those Internet sites or on other Web sites they may link to. Any comments or suggestions can be sent by e-mail to comments@enslow.com or to the address on the back cover.

Illustration Credits: Boston Public Library, p. 39; Enslow Publishers, Inc., pp. 7, 13, 24; Imperial War Museum, London, pp. 42–43; John Singer Sargent, *Dr. Pozzi at Home,* 1881. Oil on canvas, 79-3/8 x 40-1/4 inches. The Armand Hammer Collection, UCLA Hammer Museum, Los Angeles, p. 18; John Singer Sargent in his Paris studio, ca. 1885. Photographs of Artists in their paris studios 1880–1890, Archives of American Art, Smithsonian Institution, p. 15; John Singer Sargent, Self Portrait, 1892. Oil on canvas, 21 x 17 inches. National Academy of Design, New York, pp. 2, 5; Library of Congress, pp. 35, 40; The Metropolitan Museum of Art, Arthur Hoppock Hearn Fund, 1916. (16.53) Photograph c. 1997 The Metropolitan Museum of Art, p. 21; The Metropolitan Museum of Art, Bequest of Edith Minturn Phelps Stokes (Mrs. I.N.), 1938, (38.104) Photograph c. 1992 The Metropolitan Museum of Art, p. 33; Sterling and Francine Clark Art Institute, Williamstown, Massachusetts, p. 11; Tate Gallery, London, Great Britain/Art Resource, NY, p. 27; The White House Collection, Copyright White House Historical Association, p. 36.

Cover Illustration: John Singer Sargent, Self Portrait, 1892. Oil on canvas, 21 x 17 inches. National Academy of Design, New York

Contents

1 A Child in Europe 5

2 Studying Art 10

3 Madame X 14

4 Sitting for Sargent 26

In the Studio: Sargent at Work . . . 32

5 No More Portraits! 34

Timeline 44

Words to Know 45

Find Out More—Internet Addresses . . 46

Index 48

Chapter 1

A Child in Europe

John Singer Sargent, one of America's most famous painters, did not even see America until he was twenty years old. He was so talented that he made painting look easy, but he worked hard at painting every day of his life. He was very shy, but everyone who met him thought he was charming.

John was born on January 12, 1856, in Florence, Italy. His parents, FitzWilliam and Mary, had gone to Europe after their first child, a daughter, died. John's father thought they would stay away from America for just a little while, until Mary felt better. But they never moved back.

John and his younger sisters, Emily and Violet, spent their entire childhood in Europe. They moved often. In the winter, the family went someplace warm, such as Italy or southern France. In the summer, they found a cooler spot, such as the mountains of Switzerland or Germany.

The children quickly grew used to different countries and different languages. By the time John was a teenager, he could speak French, German, and Italian nearly as well as English.

John felt comfortable in all the countries of Europe. But he never really felt at home in any of them. Mostly that was because he never stayed in one place long enough to make any close friends.

Usually, John played by himself or with Emily. He liked running around outdoors a lot more than sitting inside and studying. School might have been

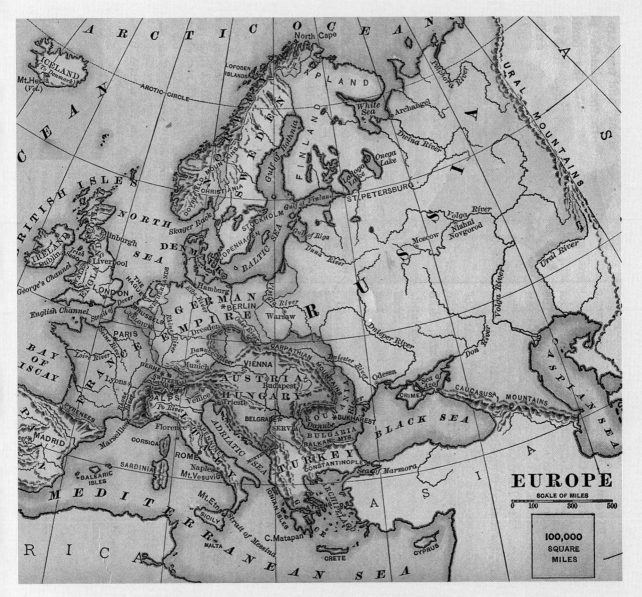

John Singer Sargent was an American citizen who was born in Europe and spent most of his life there. As a child, he moved about often, spending summers in cool Switzerland, winters in warm Italy.

a big problem for him—if he had gone. Luckily for him, his parents and tutors taught him at home. His father was his teacher for reading, science, and math. His mother taught him music and art.

Mothers usually know quite a lot about their children, and John's mother was no exception. But even she could not know that John would one day become a great artist. By chance, though, she taught him to be one.

Mary Sargent told her son to always carry a sketchbook with him. She asked him to draw whatever he saw, from city scenes to country landscapes. He drew the crashing waves of the ocean and the flowing waves of tall grass in the field. He drew almost every place he ever lived in or visited, every hillside, every beach, every town square.

John learned to amuse himself by drawing instead of playing with friends, and he got into the habit of drawing for many hours every day. It was a habit he had for his entire life. He also learned to entertain himself with music. This was in the days before there were any CDs, tapes, or even radio. To hear music, someone had to play an instrument. John wanted to hear music often, and so he became an excellent pianist.

Chapter 2

Studying Art

John's parents did not plan for him to become an artist or a musician. They thought that all children should learn to draw and play music, just as they should learn to read and write. But as John grew older, he realized that he wanted to make art all the time. When he was eighteen, he decided that it was time he learned how to be a real artist. He went to study in Paris, the center of the art world.

In Paris, John Singer Sargent went to a school that was run by the artist Carolus-Duran.

Sargent painted this wonderful portrait of his teacher in Paris, the well-known artist Carolus-Duran (1837–1917).

Sargent's teacher recognized his talent right away, and so did the other students. Sargent's paintings were the best in the school, and he quickly became one of his teacher's favorites.

Art schools are like other schools. Students often resent the teacher's favorite. So it would not have been surprising if Sargent's classmates had disliked him. Most of the other students actually liked him, though. They admired his hard work.

As Sargent studied with Carolus-Duran, he began to focus on portraits—paintings of people. This turned out to be something Sargent was especially good at doing. He was able to capture someone's personality in a single painting. The people in his paintings look like they have just stopped for a moment to tell us a quick story.

When he was twenty years old and still an art student, Sargent finally saw the United States. His mother thought it was a good time for a visit. It was 1876, and that Fourth of July was the country's one-hundredth birthday. He met his uncles, aunts, and cousins for the first time. This was the first of many visits to America for Sargent. Sometimes he would stay for more than a year, but he never stayed for good. He always went back to Europe.

Henry G. Marquand, (between 1900 and 1912). Sargent was good at many kinds of painting but was, and still is, best known for his portraits. He made a good living painting pictures of wealthy people for many years.

Chapter 3

Madame X

In Paris at that time, all the artists tried to get their paintings into a huge show called the Salon. The Salon was held every May. For the artists, this was the most important event of the year. The Salon was enormous—room after room jam-packed with art, with sculptures crowding the floors and paintings climbing the walls right up to the ceiling. Thousands of people came to see the artworks exhibited, and the artists all hoped they would be noticed and launched into stardom.

Sargent had paintings in the Salon by the time he was twenty-one, and they were noticed right away. All the critics predicted a

This photo shows Sargent in his studio in his Paris home in approximately 1884, two years before he settled in London. Just behind Sargent is the famous portrait *Madame X,* which was not well thought of in Paris. In fact, it almost caused a riot at the Salon of 1884!

great future for him. When Sargent was twenty-three, he exhibited a portrait of his teacher. The painting was so good that Carolus-Duran realized there was nothing more he could teach Sargent. It was time for Sargent to go out on his own.

Sargent had certainly grown up. He was about six feet tall, broad-shouldered, and serious-looking. He had a full beard and moustache. He made a point of dressing like a grown-up, too. Unlike some of the other students, he wore a jacket, vest, and tie all the time, even when he painted.

Sargent painted portraits for two reasons: He was good at it, and he enjoyed it. But he also wanted to make money. And in the 1880s, many people were happy to pay to have their portraits painted. A portrait made them seem important. It showed other people that they were rich and powerful. Naturally, they were eager to have the best artists paint them. Just as naturally, they usually were not eager for the artists to be completely true to reality. They often told the artists just how they wanted to look when the painting was done.

The men thought they should look solid, serious, and dependable. They thought their wives should look beautiful and their children smart and well-behaved. Mostly, they wanted to look like all the other rich people they knew. They did not want to look unusual in any way.

Sargent wanted to make these people happy. He needed them, and their wealthy friends, to hire him to paint their portraits. So he tried to make them appear as they wished. But he could not help being attracted to whatever was out of the ordinary.

Dr. Pozzi at Home (1881–1882). When Sargent was just starting to make his living as a painter, he wanted to be sure people noticed his work. Painting a man in a flowing red robe and a frilly collar and cuffs certainly must have helped.

In 1879, for example, Sargent went on a long trip to Spain to search for exotic people and places to paint. From Spain he traveled to North Africa. He went to Morocco and Tunisia. He traveled for days on horseback to reach a small village just because he had heard it was full of interesting buildings. He drew and painted everything he saw.

In these paintings he tried to do more than just paint what things looked like. He wanted people to know what it felt like to walk on a hot, dusty Moroccan dirt street or to sit in a dim café in Spain, watching a beautiful young woman dance. He wanted people to imagine the rhythm of the guitars and to hear the sound of the dancer's feet on the wooden floor.

Back in Paris, people liked Sargent's paintings of Spain. (The French did not mind if people in

Spain looked unusual.) But Sargent's fondness for exotic people got him into trouble when he met a woman named Virginie Gautreau.

She was twenty-three and, like Sargent, was an American. But she had lived in France since she was four years old. In her own way, Madame Gautreau was a celebrity. She did not actually do anything—she did not sing or dance, for example, or write or paint. But everyone knew her. You could not help noticing her. She went out of her way to look strange and mysterious. She made her pale skin even paler with lots of white powder. Then she added rose-colored makeup to her ears.

As soon as Sargent saw Virginie Gautreau, he wanted to paint her. He was sure a painting of her would make him famous. And he was right. The portrait he painted of her was his most famous

Virginie Gautreau gave Sargent so much trouble over this painting that years later, when he sold it to the Metropolitan Museum in New York, he removed her name from it. He called it simply *Madame X*.

painting. But it was also his biggest headache.

Sargent thought the painting would take him three weeks. Instead, it took months. From the start, Madame Gautreau caused him many problems. First, she would not hold still. Then, he could not find a good pose for her. He drew her sitting, kneeling, reading, playing piano. Nothing seemed right to him.

In the end, he painted her standing, with her head twisted to the side to show off her ear and nose. She wore a black dress, which made her skin look even whiter. The dress was long on the bottom but short on top. It left her pale arms, neck, and shoulders bare.

When he was finished, the painting was certainly hard to ignore. Unfortunately, to many people, it was ugly.

People were wildly upset when they saw the painting at the Paris Salon of 1884. Virginie Gautreau hated it. So did her mother, who stormed over to Sargent's studio and yelled at him. She thought the portrait made her daughter look disgraceful. She was sure that it made people want to laugh at them. Many of those who saw it agreed.

Part of the problem was her dress. The French have a word for this kind of dress: risqué, which means a bit risky. People thought the dress showed too much bare skin. When Sargent first painted it, it was even riskier: He painted the right strap slipping off Madame Gautreau's shoulder (the viewer's left), so it seemed that the dress would fall down. To calm her mother, Sargent repainted the strap on the shoulder.

Sargent moved to London in 1886. It was more or less his home for the rest of his life, though he did continue to travel quite a bit. This photo shows the famous London Bridge in 1907.

The French newspapers made quite a fuss over the portrait. For a long time it was all anyone talked about when they saw Sargent. Finally, he could not stand it anymore, and he left Paris to stay in London for a while. In 1886, when he was thirty, he moved there for good. He thought the English might like his paintings more than the French did. He was right. He soon was busy painting portraits of the rich and famous of England. London became his home for the rest of his life.

Chapter 4

Sitting for Sargent

Posing for Sargent could be difficult. He needed to please not only the people paying for the painting but also himself. Sargent always wanted his paintings to be perfect, so he made his subjects try many different poses. He had them change their clothes again and again. A person might have to pose every day for weeks and weeks before Sargent was satisfied.

Children enjoyed watching him. Although Sargent never married and had no children

Ena and Betty, Daughters of Asher and Mrs. Wertheimer (1901). Sargent painted twelve portraits of the Wertheimers over ten years.

of his own, he knew how to keep them interested. Sometimes he would dance for them or play the banjo.

It was a good thing he could keep the children happy. They had to be just as patient as the adults while sitting. One child had to pose eighty-three times before the painting of her was finished.

Sargent's paintings were an enormous success. By the 1890s he was the most famous portrait painter in England and the United States.

In 1898, he did twenty portraits. A portrait could easily require about forty sittings. The jobs began taking up all of his time.

Most of his portraits were of women. All were rich and many were either famous themselves or were married to famous men. Part of the portrait artist's job was to make his models look even more beautiful and more confident than perhaps they really were. Another part of it was to surround them with objects of value and class. But Sargent had the unusual ability to show a person's personality in the portrait as well.

Some of the famous men Sargent painted were the American writers Henry James and Robert Louis Stevenson, French artist Claude Monet, and Frederick Law Olmstead (who designed New York's Central Park). He did portraits for many members of England's aristocracy—that is, people with titles such as duke, baron, earl, or lord.

Most of the people Sargent painted were very rich. They lived in a world of huge houses and servants. But they did not all exactly belong to the same world. Some, like the Wertheimer family, were "outsiders."

Even though the Wertheimers were a large, wealthy family, they were not really accepted as part of English high society. That was because they were Jewish. At the time, not everyone in England thought Jews should be treated as equals.

Sargent, however, liked the Wertheimers. He did not pay much attention to their being Jewish. He saw them as people who were interesting to paint and fun to be with. Perhaps Sargent felt at ease with the Wertheimers because he always saw himself as an outsider also. His portraits of them are among the best he ever did. They are bright and lively. He especially liked one of the daughters, Ena (short for Helena). She became a friend of his for the rest of his life.

Not all his subjects were as pleasant as the Wertheimers. Some fussed and fidgeted. Some whined and whimpered and pouted as well as any six-year-old. They complained about how long Sargent took to finish the painting. They found little things they did not like. They asked Sargent to change the way their mouth looked, or their eyes. Sargent sometimes needed a lot of patience not to get too annoyed. And after many years of painting portraits, he found it harder and harder.

Sargent did more than five hundred portraits in all. He influenced an entire generation of portrait artists. He documented the rich and famous people of his day. It is interesting to look back and see how people saw themselves at that time.

Sargent at Work

Posing for Sargent could be difficult, but it could also be lots of fun. While he painted, he would tell stories. Sometimes, if he thought the person needed to relax, he would just stop painting. He would go over to the piano and play and sing.

Besides, it was fun just to watch him paint. Sometimes he would hum or whistle while he worked. Sometimes he would stand still, looking. Then he would back up. He would stare and think, stare and think. Then all of a sudden, he would put some paint on his brush, yell, and charge at the painting like a bull. He would make a few quick marks on the painting. Then he would stop and stare again.

Mr. and Mrs. Isaac Newton Phelps Stokes (1897). Sargent first painted the wife alone, with her hand resting on a Great Dane. When her husband insisted on being included, Sargent removed the Dane and added the hat.

Chapter 5

No More Portraits!

In 1907, when Sargent was fifty-one, he decided he had had enough. No more portraits, he promised himself. He did not need the money. By painting hundreds of portraits of the rich, he had become rich himself. He had also become so famous that King Edward VII of England wanted to make him a knight. He politely said no. To accept the honor, he would have to give up being a citizen of the United States, and Sargent would not do that. He might

Bedouins (1905). In late 1905, Sargent traveled to Syria and Palestine. Bedouins are people who move from place to place, sleep in tents, and typically own sheep and goats. They often wear colorful robes and head scarves.

live in England, but he always thought of himself as an American. Sargent now wanted to spend the rest of his life working on paintings he thought were more important than portraits.

He could not keep his promise completely. There were some people to whom he just could not say no. He felt he had to paint United States presidents Theodore Roosevelt (in 1903) and Woodrow Wilson (in 1916) when he was asked. (Who could say no to the president of the United States?) And he painted a portrait of industrialist John D. Rockefeller. (Who could say no to one of

Theodore Roosevelt (1903–1904). Even though it was a great honor to be asked to paint a portrait of a president, Sargent did not want to. But he did it. He found painting President Roosevelt very unpleasant. He said he felt like he was being ordered around all the time. This became the official White House portrait of Theodore Roosevelt.

the richest men in the world?) But even Rockefeller had to almost beg Sargent to do it before he said yes.

Mostly, though, Sargent spent the rest of his life working on other kinds of paintings. He spent many years on an enormous project for the new public library in Boston, painting a huge picture on the library ceiling. He had begun working on it in 1890. He worked on it on and off for thirty years, traveling back and forth between the United States and England.

The library painting was different from all the other work Sargent had done. In the portraits and in the paintings and drawings he did while traveling, Sargent painted real people and real places. But for the library painting he thought he could do more. He called his painting *The Triumph of Religion*.

Frieze of Prophets, North wall (installed 1895). This painting is among the murals Sargent painted in the Boston Public Library between 1890 and 1919. This work is very different from his portraits—much more fussy and, Sargent thought, much more important. But today, most people disagree.

Spanish Soldiers (1903). Sargent probably painted this watercolor during his trip to Spain in 1903. At the time, art buyers did not take watercolors very seriously. Sargent was one of several great artists in the early 1900s who changed people's minds about that.

He thought he could show thousands of years of history in one painting. This time, he was not painting people as they really lived. He was trying to use pictures to tell a long, complicated story.

Today, most people agree that the library work was not Sargent's best. John Singer Sargent was a great painter. But he did not always realize what he was best at doing.

In 1916, Sargent was hired by the Museum of

Fine Arts in Boston to paint murals inside their building and create sculptures. He worked on the museum project during the remaining years of his life. Fortunately, Sargent always did many things at the same time. During World War I, the British government asked him to do a painting of British and American soldiers fighting side by side. Sargent agreed. The only problem was that he had no idea what war really looked like. So he went to France, where the battle was raging, to find out.

What he saw changed his idea of what he should paint. He saw a long line of soldiers, standing outside, waiting to see a doctor. They were all bandaged and hurt. The Germans had used a poison gas that burned the soldiers' eyes and skin. Sargent called his painting *Gassed*. It is twenty feet long and shows more than sixty soldiers.

Gassed was one of Sargent's last great paintings. John Singer Sargent died seven years later, on April 15, 1925, at the age of sixty-nine.

When he died, newspapers in both England and the United States ran front-page stories about him. The British papers called him a great British painter.

Newspapers in the United States called him a great American painter.

Both were right. He always called himself an American. But he spent far less time in America than in England. In truth, though, he did not really live in either place. He lived to paint, wherever he was.

Gassed (1918). This painting helped people understand the horror of war. It is very big, measuring 20 feet across.

Timeline

1856 Born in Florence, Italy.

1874 Goes to Paris to study with Carolus-Duran.

1876 Visits United States for first time.

1877 Has first show at the Paris Salon.

1879 Exhibits portrait of teacher and starts life as a professional painter. Travels to Spain.

1884 Exhibits portrait of Virginie Gautreau (*Madame X*).

1885 Visits England.

1886 Makes London his permanent home.

1890 Begins Boston Public Library paintings.

1907 Announces that he will paint "no more portraits."

1914 Start of World War I.

1918 Visits battlefield in France. Paints *Gassed*.

1925 Dies in London.

Words to Know

critics — People who study or collect or write about art and who judge which art is "good" and which art is not.

exotic — Very unusual and exciting, often from another country.

high society — People who are important, wealthy, or related to royalty and generally have a lot of influence over the fashions, tastes, and opinions in their country.

portrait — A painting of a particular person, usually focused on the face.

pose — The position a person must stay in while an artist tries to make a picture or sculpture of him or her.

the Salon — The huge art exhibition that was held every year in Paris during the nineteenth century.

tutor — A private teacher, often one who comes to a student's home.

John Singer Sargent

Internet Addresses

The best way to learn more about any artist, including John Singer Sargent, is to see the art—the real thing, not just photographs of it. That is easy if you happen to live in a large city with a large art museum, such as New York or Boston. But if you do not, try the Internet. The Web sites for Sargent listed on the next page were written for people of all ages, so the text may be a bit too hard for you to get through. That is okay, though—you are just visiting for the pictures.

The John Singer Sargent Virtual Gallery For the biggest collection of Sargent's paintings on the Internet, stop into The John Singer Sargent Virtual Gallery. You will find many hundreds of his paintings here, including his best works. http://www.jssgallery.org

The Museum of Fine Arts in Boston In the past couple of years, there have been two large shows of Sargent's paintings. One was at the Museum of Fine Arts in Boston, in the summer of 1999. The show is now over, but you can still visit it online at

http://www.boston.com/mfa/sargent

Metropolitan Museum of Art The other show was held in the summer of 2000, when one of the world's great museums, The Metropolitan Museum of Art in New York, exhibited a large show of Sargent's watercolors called "John Singer Sargent Beyond the Portrait Studio: Paintings, Drawings, and Watercolors from the Collection." You can see a nice selection of the work by going to

http://www.metmuseum.org/special/sargent/john_images.htm

Index

B
Bedouins, 34–35
Boston Public Library, 38–40

C
Carolus-Duran, 10–12, 16

D
Dr. Pozzi at Home, 18

F
Frieze of Prophets, 39

G
Gassed, 41–43
Gautreau, Virginie, 20–23

H
Henry G. Marquand, 13

J
James, Henry, 29

L
London, 24, 25

M
Madame X, 15, 21–23, 25
Monet, Claude, 29
Morocco, 19
Mr. and Mrs. Isaac Newton Phelps Stokes, 33
Museum of Fine Arts, Boston, 40–41

O
Olmstead, Frederick Law, 29

P
Paris, 10, 14, 19, 25

R
Rockefeller, John D., 37
Roosevelt, Theodore, 36–37

S
Salon, the (in Paris), 14, 15
Sargent, Emily (sister), 6
Sargent, FitzWilliam (father), 5
Sargent, Mary (mother), 5, 8
Sargent, Violet (sister), 6
Spain, 19–20
Spanish Soldiers, 40
Stevenson, Robert Louis, 29

T
Triumph of Religion, The, 38
Tunisia, 19

W
Wertheimer family, 26–27, 29–30
Wilson, Woodrow, 37